PLANT MEDICINE

A guide for home use

by Charlotte Mitchell M.N.I.M.H.

Published by
Amberwood Publishing Ltd
Park Corner, Park Horsley, East Horsley, Surrey KT24 5RZ
Tel: 01483 570821

PLANTLIFE

The Natural History Museum, Cromwell Road, London SW7 5BD

Registered Charity No. 328576

Amberwood Publishing supports the Plantlife Charity,
Britain's only charity exclusively dedicated to saving wild plants.

ISBN 1-899308-13-X

Cover design by Howland Northover

Typeset and designed by
Word Perfect, Christchurch, Dorset.

Printed in Great Britain

CONTENTS

Note to Reader

Charlotte Mitchell

Charlotte Mitchell is a Medical Herbalist and was trained by the National Institute of Medical Herbalists. She qualified and was admitted for membership of the Institute in 1986 and in the same year gained her certificate in remedial massage. In 1994 Charlotte also qualified in Chinese Herbal Medicine and spent several months in China for clinical practice. She has been successfully practicing as a Medical Herbalist in Norfolk for 9 years and has also written *A Manual of Herbal Remedies* for practicing aromatherapists.

Charlotte would like to thank her family and friends for all their help and encouragement during the preparation of this book and Martin Watt for his invaluable assistance in researching scientific aspects of the work.

Introduction to the Guide

Plant Medicine – a guide to home use provides the reader with an introduction to Plant Medicine. It is designed to give an insight into the wonderful healing properties of plants.

The book gives details of the traditional uses of herbs, wherever possible supported by scientific information.

Research by NASA has shown plants to have a thera-peutic effect simply by their existence in the environment. As scientific knowledge increases, the importance of plant medicine in normalising the body's functions becomes more and more evident. It is hoped that by reference to the descriptions of herbs, advice concerning purchase, preparation and storage, as well as the clearly detailed recipes, the book might come to be used as an effective guide and make a valuable contribution to family health.

1 | History of Herbal Medicine

"Do plants and herbs really help in the treatment of disease?

"This is a surprising question because it is not so many years ago that herbal remedies were the only effective weapon in the Armoury of the Physician. Even today, naturally occurring remedies are of paramount importance in our fight against disease . . .

"For example

"Digoxin from Digitalis lanata (Foxgloves)

This drug is used for the treatment of congestive heart failure. Although it has been an established remedy for 200 years, no synthetics are available to replace it . . .

"Quinine from Cinchona spp

A specific for Malaria. Some years ago this drug was partly replaced by synthetic modifications but due to resistance of the Malaria parasite particularly in the Far East, the use of Quinine has been resumed . . ."[1]

Pharmaceutical companies worldwide, continue their research for new compounds from plants in the development of drugs. For thousands of years people throughout the world have practised healing using plant medicine. The Chinese have a relatively unbroken tradition of Herbal Medicine stretching back almost 5 thousand years to Shen-Nung Emperor of China 2838-2698BC. Furthermore, archaeologists excavating the ancient Babylonian civilisation discovered records which made extensive reference to medicinal plants. The Egyptians were also highly skilled in the art of perfumery. Some of their recipes have survived for 3,500 years in the Ebers papyri. The Greek, Hippocrates (460-377BC) is known as the 'Father of Medicine'. A physician, who travelled far and wide in researching plant medicines, Hippocrates' herbal, lists over 400 remedies many of which are in common use to this day. Early Anglo-Saxon knowledge of healing herbs was gained by word of mouth and the records sparse. However, some information has been preserved in the writings of Roman observers. The Romans introduced many herbs into

---

1. A quotation extracted from an article written by F.J. Evans, B.Pharm., Ph.D., M.P.S., F.L.S. in the 'New Herbal Practitioner' Nov. 1975.

England which formed the basis of 'physick gardens' created by medieval monks who ran hospitals in the monasteries. After 1600AD several seminal works were published by practitioners with a working knowledge of herbs. Master Surgeon, John Gerrard (1545-1607) produced his well known herbal entitled, 'The Herball' or 'General Historie of Plantes'. Similarly, Culpepper (1616-1654), whose life's work included many interesting herbal essays, practised from Spitalfields in London and treated many people. In the 19th century Dr Albert Coffin brought herbal medicine to the working classes in England who could not afford other medical treatment and as a result numerous American plants were incorporated into the Materia medica and are still used in herbal practice. During the last War many medicines had to be produced from our own wild or cultivated plants. This stimulated a revival in the use of plant medicines which has continued and blossomed today.

The following, outlines some of the important regulatory landmarks in the development of herbal medicine.

1548 – Henry VIII's Act 1548 or the so called 'Quacks Charter' came at a time when Surgeons were intent on stamping out the practice of Herbal Medicine by those who, despite their wide knowledge and experience, had no formal recognition within the established Medical profession. This Act has been of paramount importance in the survival of Medical Herbalists, and is part of British common law under which they still work.

1968 – Medicines Act. Following the Thalidomide tragedy in the early 1960s this Act was designed to tighten controls governing the sale of medicinal substances and to improve clinical trials.

1971 – Existing Medical products on the market at the time, not considered hazardous, were required to be registered and were given 'product licences of right' in 1971. In the following years all such products were required to be fully reviewed to assess their purity, safety and efficacy. Herbal medicines were also subject to this review in order to gain full product licences. This work was completed in the UK, in conformity with EC directives, by 1991.

1991 – Today it is recognised that the careful investigation and monitoring of the safety and effectiveness of plants is useful and in some cases essential but empirical knowledge must also be considered when judging the safety and efficacy of particular plants.

EC legislation confirms the position of plant medicine, giving it the status and position to maintain the availability of these substances into the 21st Century.

2 | Guide for self treatment

1) It is important to remember that for effective and long lasting treatment the cause of a problem or illness must be sought and dealt with. For example.

Q. *What is causing your migraine?*
Tension
Hormonal factors
Certain foods
Is it being aggravated by irregular eating habits or an unbalanced diet?

A. Select the possible cause(s) and treat with the recommended plant.

Q. *Do you suffer from repeated infections?*

A. If you are under a lot of stress or suffering from tiredness, add relaxant or tonic herbs to those used to strengthen the immune system and you may not reach the stage of needing to make up a gargle to soothe your sore throat!

Refer to plants used to treat specific ailments under stress, tiredness and immune system.

In an ideal situation it would be possible to rely on plants as prophylactics i.e. to prevent illness. However, disease does exist; plants used in herbal medicines are both effective in treating diseases as well as maintaining health. Many of the plants used exert a balancing or normalising effect on body functions and encourage the body's natural healing powers.

2) Herbal medicine has been found to be more effective when tea, coffee and alcohol are **reduced** in the diet.

GUIDELINES ON SELECTING A TREATMENT

i) Refer to 'Plants for Specific Ailments' (page 14) to select the individual plants.
ii) Look under the 'A–Z of Medicinal Plants' (page 23) for the necessary information on the one/s selected.

iii) Check under 'Warnings and Cautions' (page 55).

iv) Turn to 'Making the Most of Plants' (page 11) and follow the relevant procedure.

How to use the plants

For 'Methods of preparation' see pages 12-13.

For 'Recipes' see pages 58-60.

DOSAGE of the plants

> *Adults:* General: See 'Making the most of plants' page 11.
> Specific: see individual plants in the 'A-Z of Medicinal Plants'.
>
> *Children:* 1-6 years of age – a third of the adult dose.
> 6-15 years of age – half the adult dose.

Note: All specific dosages refer to the amount of dried plant material.

DOSAGE of essential oils

> *Adults:* See 'Making the most of plants' and individual plants in the 'A-Z of Medicinal Plants'.
>
> *Children:* 6-12 years of age – half the adult dose.
> External dose only.
> 12-15 years of age – normal adult.

TIME OF TREATMENT

This is a complex matter but those herbs where time is of particular importance are:

> *Appetite stimulants* – take BEFORE food.
> *Slippery elm* – take BEFORE food.
> *Ginseng* – take on an empty stomach mid-morning.

LENGTH OF TREATMENT

Do not expect instant relief in all cases. Plants can take a little time to have their full effect e.g. scientific experiments using extracts of chamomile have demonstrated that when it is applied to the skin to treat irritation and inflammation its excellent healing properties take effect very slowly and are most pronounced after the first 24 hours.

THE INDIVIDUAL RESPONSE

Everybody is unique. Remember this when selecting your plants. Certain plants may suit you better or be more appropriate for you than others.

PREGNANCY
Refer to individual section, page 53.

Making the most of plants
Here are some tips on the purchase, gathering, storage and preparation of plants.

Plant parts
Different parts of plants have specific medicinal properties, e.g.;

Parts Used	Examples of Plants	Example of Properties
Leaves	Sage	Antiseptic
Flowers (whole)	Chamomile	Relaxant
Petals	Marigold	Wound healing
Fruits	Vitex agnus castus	Hormone regulator
Seeds	Fennel	Carminative
Whole plant above ground (Aerial parts)	Nettle	Tonic/Nutritive
Bark	Slippery elm	Nutritive
Roots	Ginger	Anti-nausea
Bulbs	Garlic	Immune stimulant
Tubers	Devil's claw	Anti-inflammatory
Essential oil	Lavender	Anti-depressant

Fresh Plants
Before using fresh plants check under 'Gathering Herbs' in warnings and cautions (page 55) and under individual plants in the 'A-Z of Medicinal Plants' (page 23) for those few that are unsuitable.

Procedure
1) Cut enough material for one cup of 'tea' or at the most, sufficient for a couple of days.
2) Cut off dead and imperfect parts.
3) Wash well in clean cold water.
4) Shake or dry on paper towels.
5) Use immediately.

Purchasing Plant Materials
To ensure the herbs are of the highest quality, it is essential to purchase them from a reputable supplier. They may be obtained as the loose dried herb, as teabags or processed in the form of tablets and capsules.

Storage
The plants are best kept in air tight glass jars in a dry, cool, dark place for up to a year. Brown paper bags can be used for storage, again keep in a dry place but do not store with clothing.

Methods of preparation for INTERNAL use
For internal use there are two basic methods: infusion and decoction. Both work by extracting active plant constituents with water.

INFUSION
Plant parts most suitable:-
Leaves	*Suitable containers*
Petals	Teapot (avoid aluminium or tin)
Flowers	cup
Seeds (bruised or ground)	thermos flask
Bark or root (powdered or chopped if fresh)	jug (not plastic)

Method
Rinse the pot with boiling water to warm it. Place required amount of herb in pot and add sufficient boiling water. (It is important with aromatic plants such as peppermint, lavender, rosemary, chamomile to use hot, not boiling water and to cover the container quickly to prevent loss of essential oils.) Replace lid or cover and leave to infuse for 10-15 mins. Strain. Either drink 1 cup 3 times a day or gargle with a small cupful at frequent intervals.

DECOCTION
Plant parts most suitable:-	*Suitable containers*
Seeds (bruised)	Saucepan (not aluminium)
Bark (broken into small pieces or crushed)	
Roots (broken into small pieces or crushed) or chopped if fresh	

Method
Put required amount of herb and cold water in a saucepan. Cover and bring to the boil. Reduce heat and allow to simmer for 10-15 mins. Strain and drink 1 cup 3 times a day or gargle with a small cupful at frequent intervals.

General dosage (but for specific dose see individual plants)
Dried plant – To make a single cup of tea, use 1 heaped tsp of the dried herb to 1 cupful of boiling water. For a larger quantity, use 30gms (1oz) to ½ ltr. (1pt). Fresh plant – Three times that of dried.
Essential oils – See under external use.

12

Keeping infusions/decoctions
Infusions and decoctions last a couple of days if kept in the 'fridge in suitable containers, e.g. jug, jar.

Crushing/grinding
Place plant in a clean cloth. Crush with a rolling pin or grind in an electric grinder.
N.B. Bark and roots may be too hard and cause damage to the grinder.

Methods of preparation for EXTERNAL use

LOTION
Make an infusion or decoction, allow to cool then strain and apply externally as a rub or dab using cotton wool or tissue, repeat application as necessary.

COMPRESS
Make an infusion or decoction, soak a piece of linen, gauze, muslin or cotton wool pad in the liquid and apply as hot as possible to the troublesome area. Leave until it has cooled. Repeat as necessary.

POULTICE
Stir enough powdered herb into a small quantity of boiling water to make a paste like consistency. Apply directly or spread between two layers of muslin or gauze and apply to the affected area. Use as hot as possible. Remove when cold. This may be repeated several times. A hot water bottle placed over the poultice will keep it warm for longer.

ESSENTIAL OILS AS A RUB
Only purchase from a reputable supplier. Always dilute in good quality vegetable oil (sweet almond, fractionated coconut, sunflower, jojoba, peach kernel, olive, safflower) unless otherwise stated. Mix 2-3 drops of essential oils in every 5mls of vegetable oil. Use a glass container when mixing oils, do not use your crockery, or it will be contaminated with the smell and taste of the oil. Store mixed essential oils in dark, glass bottles in a cool place.

EYE BATH
Make an infusion or decoction, allow to cool then strain and filter through filter paper, or several layers of strong new tissue, this is vital to ensure all the plants fibres and other particles are removed.

3 | Plants for specific ailments

Symbols Key

a	EXTERNAL APPLICATION AS A RUB
b	BATH
c	CAPSULES
co	COMPRESS
d	DECOCTION
e	EYEBATH
f	FOOD
i	INFUSION
l	LOTION
p	POULTICE
t	TABLETS
s	SYRUP
g	GARGLE
tsp	TEASPOON
tbsp	TABLESPOON

ANXIETY	Chamomile	i b
	Damiana	i c/t
	Hops	c/t i
	Motherwort	i c/t
	St John's Wort	i c/t
	Valerian	d c/t
APPETITE ENHANCER	Golden Seal	c/t g
	Dandelion: *leaf*	f i
	Hops	i c/t
ARTHRITIS	Black Cohosh	c/t
	Celery: *stem*	f
	Celery: *seed*	c/t i/d
	Garlic	f c/t
	Nettle	i f
	Feverfew	f t/c
	Dandelion: *leaf & root*	i/d f c/t
	Devils Claw	d c/t

For an arthritic rub, see Recipe No. 11.
Arthritis is a general name given to a number of conditions.
Nutritional advice may help but complex factors contribute to
these diseases; expert advice is advantageous.

BOILS	Blue Flag	dt/c	
	Echinacea	d t/c l	
	Garlic	f t/c	
	Marigold	i l co	
	Nettle	i f	
	Slippery Elm	p	
	If stress is present, it may help to include relaxants.		
BRUISES	Marigold	l	
	Witch Hazel		
	Apply distilled		
	Witch Hazel neat)		
	Ginger	f i/d	
	If sudden onset of major bruising occurs, check with your medical practitioner		
BURNS *(minor)*	Teatree Oil		
	Lavender		
	Apply a few drops of neat oil to the area immediately.		
	Marigold	l	
CATARRH	Elderflowers	i	For essential oils, see
	Use an infusion of		Recipe No. 3 page 58
	2 teasp of flowers in a		
	small cup of hot water,		
	3-4 times daily.		
	Sage	i f	
	Thyme	i f	
	Golden Seal	c/t	
	For infective catarrh add		
	Echinacea	d/t c	
	Garlic	f t/c	
	Dietary measures may assist this condition, including increasing proportion of fresh fruit and vegetables in the diet.		
CHOLESTEROL	*Plants that have been traditionally used to reduce cholesterol levels are:*		
	Garlic	f c/t	
	Oat Bran	f t	
	Fenugreek	f i t/c	
CIRCULATION	Cayenne	f	
	(Capsicum minimum)		
	particularly during		
	winter. Add a pinch to		
	soups, stews, casseroles, etc		
	Garlic	f c/t	
	Ginger	f i/d	
	Ginkgo	t/c	
	Hawthorn	i t/c	
	Marigold	i	
	Rosemary	f i	
	Lime Blossom	i	
COLD SORES	Lemon Balm	co i	
(herpes simplex)	St John's Wort Oil	a	See St John's Wort page 48.

15

COLDS and INFLUENZA	Garlic	f c/t	
	Elderflowers		*See under catarrh.*
	Echinacea	d t/c	
	Ginger	fi/d t	*See Recipe No. 8*
	Sage	i f	
	Thyme	i f	
	Lemon Balm	i	
	Lime Blossom	i	
	Peppermint	i c f	

Infusions should be drunk as hot as possible.

CONJUNCTIVITIS	Fennel	e
	Marigold	e

If this condition persists consult a medical adviser.

CONSTIPATION	Dandelion: *root*	dt/c
	Senna	t/csi

This may be significantly helped by dietary measures such as increasing fruit, vegetables and grains and by reducing bland foods. If anxiety or tension is present, laxatives may not be fully effective, in which case the following relaxant plants should be used in place of the above:

	Chamomile	i
	Lemon Balm	i
	Lime Blossom	i
	Valerian	d t/c
	Cramp Bark	d t/c
COUGHS	Fennel	i/d
	Garlic	f c/t
	Liquorice	f d
	Sage	g
	Thyme	i g

As a guide only to the treatment of coughs. It is important to know the nature of the cough to give correct treatment. See under individual herbs for additional information.

COUGH, *nervous*	Thyme	i f
CYSTITIS	Garlic	f t/c
	Golden Seal	t/c
	Buchu	i t/c
	Celery: *seeds*	f i/d
	Uva Ursi	i t/c
	Thyme	i

If this condition persists consult a medical advisor.

DANDRUFF	Rosemary		*See Recipe No. 7*
	Rosemary Oil	a	*See herb page 47.*
	Sage		*See Recipe No. 7*
	Nettles	d	
	Teatree Oil		

Dissolve Teatree oil in a vegetable oil 50/50.
Jojoba oil, otherwise sunflower or almond. Rub into the scalp.
Do not use for more than 2-3 days.

DEPRESSION, *mild*	Damiana	i t/c	
	Lavender	i	
	Lavender Oil	b	*See page 39.*

16

DEPRESSION, *mild*		
continued	Lemon Balm	i b
	Panax Ginseng	f d c/t
	Rosemary	i b
DIARRHOEA, *mild*	Cranesbill	c/t d
	Nettles	i
	Thyme	i
	Sage	i
	Peppermint	i c

Do not merely suppress diarrhoea symptoms. Always include herbs to treat the underlying infection. Refer to 'A-Z of Medicinal Plants' Consult your medical practitioner if symptoms persist for more than a few days.

DIARRHOEA, *nervous*	Chamomile	i
	Valerian	d c/t
	Cranesbill	t/c d
	Hops	i t/c
DIGESTIVE AID	Dandelion: *leaf*	i t/c
	root	d t/c
	Fennel	d/i t/c
	Fenugreek	f d/i t/c
	Ginger	i/d f
ECZEMA	Echinacea	dc/t l
	Blue Flag	d c/t
	Nettles	i f
	Red Clover	i
	Lavender	l

It is important to discover the causative factors of eczema, e.g. 1. Various substances like bleach, washing powders and furniture polish can cause contact eczema. 2. May be linked with stress; in which case include relaxant plants.

EXAM NERVES	Panax Ginseng	d t/c
	Valerian	d t/c
EYES, *sore*	Chamomile	e
	Marigold	e
FLATULENCE, COLIC	Chamomile	i
	Cramp Bark	d t/c
	Fennel	i/d
	Ginger	f i/d t
	Lavender	i
	Peppermint	i c
	Rosemary	f i
	Thyme	f i
	Valerian	d c/t
	Wild Yam	d t/c

For flatulence also see appetite enhancers.

FRACTURES	Comfrey	i t p
GASTRITIS/ENTERITIS	Liquorice	f d t/c
	Golden Seal	t/c
	Fenugreek	f i/d t/c
	Slippery Elm	f i/d t/c

GINGIVITIS	Chamomile	g	
	Sage	g	*See Recipe No. 1 page 58.*
	Thyme	g	*See Recipe No. 1 page 58.*
	Echinacea	g	
HAIR, *to lighten*	Chamomile		*See Recipe No. 6.*
to darken	Sage		*See Recipe No. 7.*
	Rosemary		*See Recipe No. 7.*
HANDS, *sore and chapped*	Lavender Oil		*See page 59.*
HAYFEVER, *mild*	Chamomile	i	
HEADACHES, *Stress*	Chamomile	i	
	Lavender	i	
	Lavender Oil		*See Recipe No. 4.*
	Peppermint	i	
	Peppermint Oil		*See Recipe No. 4.*
	Rose Petals		*See Recipe No. 4.*
	Rosemary	i	
	Passion Flower	i t	
	Pulsatilla	i t	
	Valerian	d t/c	
	St John's Wort	i t/c	
HEADACHES, *tension*	*Associated with muscle tension of neck and shoulders.*		
	Valerian	d c/t	
	Cramp Bark	d c/t	
	Lavender Oil		*See page 39.*
HEADACHES, *influenza*	Lemon Balm	i	
	Lavender Oil		*See page 39.*
HEADACHES, *menstrual*	Valerian	dc/t	
	Lemon Balm	i	
	Additionally, see hormonal regulators under pre-menstrual syndrome.		
	If headaches are persistent, a medical advisor must be consulted.		
HAEMORRHOIDS	Golden Seal	c/t l	
	Marigold	l i	
	Chamomile	l i	
	Witch Hazel		*See under bruises.*
	Teatree Oil		
	Mix 10 drops Teatree oil into 15ml (approx 1 dessertspoon) of soft margarine. Apply a small amount once or twice a day.		
	It is important to avoid constipation. Exercise is helpful.		
INDIGESTION and	Chamomile	i t/c	
HEARTBURN	Damiana	i t/c	
	Dandelion: *leaf*	i f	
	root	d	
	Ginger	i/d f	
	Golden Seal	c/t	
	Lavender	i	

18

INDIGESTION and HEARTBURN *continued*	Liquorice	f i/d
	Peppermint	i c
	Slippery Elm	i c/t
	Fennel	d/i t/c f
	Rosemary	i f
	Thyme	i f

If symptoms persist, consult a medical advisor.

HOT FLUSHES	Motherwort	i t/c
	Sage	i
	Vitex agnus castus	i/d t
IMMUNE SYSTEM, *to boost*	Echinacea	d c/t
	Garlic	f c/t
	Panax Ginseng	f d c/t
INSOMNIA	Chamomile	i
	Hops	i c/t
	Lavender	i
	Lavender Oil	b	See page 39.
	Lemon Balm	i b
	Panax Ginseng	f d c/t
	Passion Flower	i t/c
	Valerian	d t/c
	Peppermint	i

Relaxation techniques used in conjunction with plant medicine can provide additional benefit.

IRRITABLE *nervous* BOWEL	Chamomile	i
	Cramp Bark	d c/t
	Hops	i c/t
	Wild Yam	d c/t
	Valerian	d c/t
	Peppermint	i c
	with diarrhoea include	
	Cranesbill	d c/t

It is important to note that nervous bowel can be caused by a food allergy. If this condition persists you should consult your medical practitioner.

LARYNGITIS	Sage	f i g
	Thyme	f i g
LIBIDO *(to increase) – Male*	Damiana	i c/t
	Panax Ginseng	f d c/t
LIBIDO – *(to increase) - Female*	Vitex agnus castus	d/i c/t
	Damiana	i t/c
	See also stress.	
MEMORY, to *improve*	Rosemary	i
	Ginkgo	c/t
MENOPAUSE		
Hormonal	Helonias	d
	Motherwort	i t/c
	Sage	i
	Vitex agnus castus	i/d t
	Black Cohosh	c/t

MENOPAUSE *continued*

Anxiety/tension	St John's Wort	i t c
	Black Cohosh	c/t

Also refer to herbs used for stress.

MENSTRUAL PAIN	Black Cohosh	c/t
	Chamomile	i
	Cramp Bark	d t/c
	Ginger	f i/d t/c
	Golden Seal	c t/c
	Valerian	d c/t
MIGRAINE	Feverfew	f c/t
	Ginger	f i/d t/c

Stress induced migraine:

	Pulsatilla	i t/c
	Chamomile	i
	Valerian	d c/t

Additionally see under stress.

Menstrual migraine: use Hormonal regulators + relaxant plants (see under P.M.S. and stress). General guidance: Eliminate possibility of food trigger or structural problems (consult medical herbalist, osteopath or chiropractor as appropriate). Take regular meals to avoid risk of low blood sugar levels.

MOUTH ULCERS:	Sage	g
aphthous ulcers	Marigold	g
MUSCLE TENSION	Valerian	d c/t
	Cramp Bark	d c/t
	Juniper Oil	a

Mix 1ml of Juniper Oil into 20ml of vegetable oil.

NAUSEA	Chamomile	i	
	Ginger	f i/d t/c	
	Peppermint	i f c	
	Peppermint Oil		*See pages 44-45.*
NEURALGIA and	Echinacea	l co	
SCIATICA	St John's Wort Oil	a	*See St John's Wort and Recipe No. 9.*
	Rosemary Oil	a	*See Rosemary.*
	Roman Chamomile	l	
NUTRITIONAL	Kelp	f i t/c	
	Dandelion: *leaf*	f i t/c	
	and root	d t/c	
	Slippery Elm	f i/d t/c	
	Fenugreek	f i/d t/c	
	Kelp	f t/c	
	Nettle	f i	
OVERWEIGHT	Kelp	f i t/c	
PALPITATIONS, *nervous*	Motherwort	i c/t	*See also stress herbs.*
PRE-MENSTRUAL	Damiana	i c/t	
SYNDROME	Pulsatilla	i	
	Evening Primrose oil	c	

As directed by manufacturer.

20

PRE-MENSTRUAL			
SYNDROME *continued*	Helonias	d	
	Vitex agnus castus	t i/d	
PRURITUS – *Ano-genital*	TeatreeOil		*See above as under*
irritation			*Haemorrhoids.*
General skin itching	Lavender	l	
	Chamomile	l	
SHINGLES, *pain*	*St John's Wort Oil*	a	*See St John's Wort.*
	Echinacea	l t	
	It can prove helpful to take tonic (see tiredness) and immune		
	stimulant herbs.		
SINUSITIS			*See infective catarrh*
			under catarrh.
SORE THROATS	Echinacea	g d	
(Pharyngitis)	Golden Seal	c/t g	
	Peppermint	i	
	Sage	g i	*See Recipe No. 1.*
	Thyme	i g	*See Recipe No. 1.*
	Echinacea	d t g	
STOMACH UPSETS, *minor*	Chamomile	i	
	Lemon Balm	i	
	Sage	i	
	Slippery Elm	d/i t/c	
	Thyme	i	
	Garlic	f c/t	
	Peppermint	i c	*See also Peppermint Oil.*
STOMACH UPSETS,	Hops	i c/t	
nervous			
STRESS	Chamomile	b i	
	Hops	i c/t	
	Lavender	i	
	Lavender Oil	a	*See page 39.*
	Lemon Balm	i b	
	Lime Blossom	i	
	Motherwort	i t/c	
	Valerian	d c/t	
	Panax Ginseng	f t/c	
TIREDNESS	Damiana	i t/c	
	Panax Ginseng	f c/t	
	Lavender	i	
	Kelp	f c/t	
	Nettles	f i	
	If nutritional factors involved:		
	Rosemary	b f i	
TONSILLITIS	Sage	g i	
	Echinacea	g d	
TOOTH EXTRACTION	Chamomile	g a	*See Recipe No. 1.*
(following)	Lavender Oil	a	*See Recipe No. 1.*
TRAVEL SICKNESS	Peppermint Oil		*See pages 44-45.*
	Ginger	f i/d c/t	

WOUNDS, *minor*	Comfrey: *leaf*	l/p
GRAZES, *minor*	*root*	l/p
	Echinacea	l
	St John's Wort	l
	St John's Wort Oil	a
	Marigold	l
	Thyme	l
	Nettle	l
	Slippery Elm	p

All these herbs can be used for wounds and grazes.

4 | A–Z of medicinal plants

BLACK COHOSH ~
Cimicifuga Racemosa

A North American herb. It is also known as Black Snake Root and Squaw Root.

> *Part used:*   Root
> *Specific uses:* MENSTRUAL PAIN, MENOPAUSAL TENSION, ARTHRITIS

Traditional uses and general information: Scientific information backs up Black Cohosh's traditional use by the North American Indians in regulating the menstrual cycle. It was also used to ease labour pains, menstrual cramps and anxiety associated with the menopause. The herb is helpful in the treatment of arthritis and has a history of use in chronic lung disease e.g. chronic bronchitis. A syrup of the plant can be taken as a cough remedy.

Methods of use and dosage: Tablets and capsules as directed by the manufacturer.

Precautions: Best taken as tablets/capsules. Large quantities of the herb may cause symptoms such as vomiting, vertigo and tremors. Not suitable for children.

BLUE FLAG ~
Iris versicolor L.

Blue Flag is one of the family of plants named after 'Iris'. It was so named because of the beauty and colour of the flowers.

> *Parts used:*   Roots
> *Specific uses:* ECZEMA, BOILS

BLUE FLAG ~ *continued*

Traditional uses and general information: Blue Flag is primarily a cleansing herb used in a wide range of skin conditions, e.g. psoriasis, dermatitis. It is used as a liver tonic and laxative and also taken to increase the flow of bile from the gall bladder. Blue Flag has diuretic properties and claims have been made for it as an anti-obesity agent.

Methods of use and dosage: A decoction made with ½-1 tsp of the dried root to a cup of cold water. Take 3 times daily.

Tablets and capsules, as directed by the manufacturer.

Precautions: Not suitable for children.

BUCHU ~

Agathosma betulina

This interesting and much valued plant grows wild in South Africa. The leaves are gathered for use at the flowering and fruiting stage.

> *Parts used:* Leaves
> *Specific uses:* CYSTITIS, URETHRITIS

Traditional uses and general information: Buchu's antiseptic qualities have been used to treat infections of the urinary tract and is also used to aid the flow of urine. It has been used to treat bronchitis by promoting gentle expectoration.

Methods of use and dosage: An infusion made with 1-2 tsps of Buchu in a cup of hot water. Take 3 times daily.

Tablets and capsules as directed by the manufacturer.

Precautions: Not suitable for children.

CELERY ~

Apium graveolens L.

Celery is a well known garden vegetable cultivated throughout Europe and is a plant containing valuable medicinal qualities.

> *Parts used:* (i) Stem in food
> (ii) Fruit (seed) is used in food and herbal preparations
> *Specific uses:* ARTHRITIS, CYSTITIS (the seed only)

CELERY ~ *continued*

Traditional uses and general information: Research has shown the celery stem to have anti-inflammatory properties. The seed is used to treat urinary tract infections because of its antiseptic action. It has also been taken for the relief of flatulence, colic, as a diuretic and for its sedative action. Celery seed oil has been found to be effective against certain types of fungi.

Methods of use and dosage: The stem – use as food.

The seed – an infusion made with 1-2 tsp of the ground or crushed seeds in a cup of hot water taken 3 times daily.

Tablets and capsules, as directed by the manufacturer.

Precautions: Do not use celery seed if suffering from kidney disease. Do not take during pregnancy.

Celery seed is unsuitable for children and not recommended for prolonged use.

CHAMOMILE ~

Matricaria recutita L.

Matricaria recutita is also called 'German Chamomile' although it is widely grown in many other countries.

Parts used: (i) Flower heads in herbal preparations
(ii) An essential oil extracted from the flowers is used in Aromatherapy, Perfumery and Cosmetics
Specific uses: STRESS RELIEF, STOMACH UPSETS, MILD MENSTRUAL PAIN, HAYFEVER and other ALLERGIES, STRESS HEADACHES, MIGRAINES, NERVOUS DIARRHOEA

Traditional uses and general information: A simple infusion applied to the skin will help relieve the irritation of MILD sunburn.

A paste made from the flowers will lighten hair colour (see Recipe No. 6).

It has been scientifically proven that chamomile contains several active compounds which make this plant suitable to help a wide range of ailments. The hot water from an infusion reacts with the chamomile to create a substance called azulene which research has shown to have a powerful anti-inflammatory action.

CHAMOMILE ~ *continued*
Methods of use and dosage: An infusion made with 1-2 tsp of chamomile or a chamomile teabag in a cup of hot water. Take 3-4 times daily (see Recipe section) .

To assist relaxation from stress, place two chamomile teabags in your bath water. The herb may also be included in a gargle for sore throats, gingivitis, laryngitis (see Recipe No. 1). Use the cooled lotion as an eyewash for sore eyes, (ensuring it is well filtered) and apply to itchy skin.

Tablets and capsules as directed by the manufacturer.

Precautions: Although chamomile usually has a soothing action either when taken or applied to the skin, in rare cases it may cause an allergic reaction which manifests itself as a skin rash or an area of irritation around the mouth. Should this occur, discontinue its use.

CHAMOMILE, ROMAN ~
Chamaemelum nobile
This form of chamomile used to be grown on low walls where, as ladies sat in their crinoline dresses its pleasant aroma was released.

Parts used: As for Matricaria
Specific uses: STRESS RELIEF, INDIGESTION (caused by tension)

Traditional uses and general information: It is used as a tonic, and a carminative (eases griping and flatulence). Externally it is included in anti-inflammatory creams. It has a mild sedative action and can be usefully employed as a soothing lotion for neuralgia and nappy rash. The essential oil is a transparent light green with a 'fruity top note' (a descriptive term used in perfumery).

Methods of use and dosage: An infusion made with 1-2 tsp of the dried flowers in a cup of hot water. Take 3 times daily.

Tablets and capsules as directed by the manufacturer.

CRANESBILL, AMERICAN ~
Geranium maculatum
This plant has fruit with long barbs like the beak of the crane bird from which it gets its name.

Part used: Root
Specific use: DIARRHOEA

CRANESBILL, AMERICAN ~ *continued*

Traditional uses and general information: Cranesbill is used for the short term relief of diarrhoea, or as a gargle for mouth and throat infections and following tooth extraction to prevent excessive bleeding. Use as a lotion for wounds and for the treatment of haemorrhoids. It is an effective but gentle remedy suitable for the elderly and children.

Methods of use and dosage: A decoction made with ½–2 tsp of the dried root. Take 3 times daily or as required.

Tablets and capsules as directed by the manufacturer.

COMFREY ~

Symphytum officinale

Gerard, an apothecary to James I, in his famous Herball wrote that 'Comfrey does heal all fresh and greene woundes'.

> *Parts used:* Root and leaves
> *Specific uses:* WOUNDS (minor), FRACTURES

Traditional uses and general information: A plant renowned for its healing properties. It is applied locally to promote healing of bones and to stimulate tissue repair and is taken internally to heal digestive tract ailments. A constituent 'Allantoin' is responsible for the plant's effectiveness in wound healing. It has been used for centuries as a soothing expectorant in lung complaints and for arthritis.

Comfrey can also be used as a gargle or mouthwash in the treatment of sore throats, pharyngitis and bleeding gums.

Methods of use and dosage: An infusion made with 1–2 tsps of the dried leaves in a cup of boiling water. Take 3 times daily. A decoction made with 1 tsp of the dried root in a cup of cold water. Take 3 times daily.

Tablets and capsules as directed by the manufacturer.

For fractures and minor wounds use a poultice in addition to taking tablets.

Precautions: There have been reports that taking comfrey internally can be harmful. The evidence is unconvincing. However, as a precaution, avoid excessive or long term consumption.

CRAMP BARK ~
Viburnum opulus

This shrub or small tree is a member of the honeysuckle family and is otherwise known as the guelder rose.

Part used: The stem bark
Specific uses: MUSCLE TENSION, MENSTRUAL PAIN, CONSTIPATION (caused by tension), IRRITABLE BOWEL

Traditional uses-and general information: Cramp bark is best used, in the short term, for any conditions resulting from muscle tension. The decoction can be applied locally as a rub to ease muscle tension.

Methods of use and dosage: A decoction made with 1-2 tsp of the dried bark in a cup of cold water. Take 3 times daily.

Tablets and capsules, as directed by the manufacturer.

Precautions: Not suitable for children or for prolonged use.
The berries of this plant are poisonous.

DAMIANA ~
Turnera diffusa

Damiana is a plant indigenous to Texas and Mexico and was used by the North American Indians.

Parts used: Leaves and stem
Specific uses: MILD DEPRESSION, INDIGESTION (caused by tension), ANXIETY (where sexual factor involved), TIREDNESS

Traditional uses and general information: Damiana is a tonic to the nervous and hormonal systems. It has a reputation as an aphrodisiac and is used to treat sexual debility.

Methods of use and dosage: An infusion made with 1-2 tsp of dried damiana in a cup of boiling water. Take 3 times daily.
Tablets and capsules as directed by the manufacturer.

Precautions: Not suitable for children.

DANDELION ~
Taraxacum officinale

It has been reported that during a famine on the island of Minorca all the vegetation was stripped by locusts. The inhabitants were able to survive for a time on dandelion roots due to their high nutritive value.

Parts used: Roots and leaves
Specific uses: NUTRITIONAL FOOD, APPETITE ENHANCER, DIGESTIVE AID (increases production of bile), CONSTIPATION (gentle laxative), DIURETIC

Traditional uses and general information: The roots and leaves have a similar action. However, the leaves are used more for their diuretic properties and the root for its effect on the gall bladder and liver. Dandelion may be taken as a remedy for arthritis. In France it has been used to treat chronic skin diseases. The roasted root may be taken as a substitute for coffee.

In general, when using diuretics there is a danger that with the increased urine output, too much potassium will be lost from the body. However, scientific experiments have found that the dandelion root and herb are such a good source of potassium that they provide the body with greater quantities than are eliminated.

Methods of use and dosage: Leaves – a couple of leaves each day taken in salad, or 1-2 tsp of the dried herb taken as an infusion in a cup of boiling water. Take 3 times daily.
Root – A decoction made with 1-2 teasp of dried herb in a cup of cold water. Take 3 times daily.

DEVILS CLAW ~
Harpagophytum procumbens

Named so because of its claw like fruit. This plant is a native of South West Africa.

Part used: Tuber
Specific use: ARTHRITIS

Traditional uses and general information: Devil's claw is used for its anti-inflammatory action in arthritis, myalgia and fibrositis. It is thought to have a stimulating effect on the liver, gall bladder function and on the lymphatic system.

DEVILS CLAW ~ *continued*
Methods of use and dosage: A decoction made with ½-1 tsp of dried tuber in a cup of cold water. Take 3 times daily.

Tablets and capsules as directed by the manufacturer.

Precautions: Not suitable for children.

ECHINACEA ~
Echinacea angustifotia
Echinacea pallida
Echinacea purpurea

North American Indians applied this plant as a lotion to their skin, before entering their steam lodges. It has a mild anaesthetic action thus increasing tolerance to the hot steam.

> *Part used:* Root
> *Specific uses:* COLDS, INFLUENZA, NASAL CATARRH, SINUSITIS, GINGIVITIS, TONSILLITIS, SORE THROATS, PHARYNGITIS, ECZEMA, BOILS, NEURALGIA (external), SHINGLES (external)

Traditional uses and general information: Today medical herbalists give Echinacea internally to stimulate the body's immune system, i.e. its ability to resist and fight infection and as a cleansing herb to treat various skin conditions, e.g. boils and acne. Its anti-viral and antibacterial properties have been successfully, scientifically investigated. Externally, it may be applied as a poultice to encourage the healing of wounds.

Methods of use and dosage: A decoction made with 1-2 tsp of the dried root in a cup of cold water. Take this decoction 3 times daily.

Tablets and capsules as directed by the manufacturer.

A decoction, used as a gargle or mouthwash for sore throats, tonsillitis, pharyngitis and gingivitis in conjunction with internal use.

Apply a lotion or compress to neuralgia + shingles, (avoid eye area).

FENNEL ~
Foeniculum vulgare

In Ancient Greece Fennel was an emblem of victory. They named it 'marathon' to commemorate their famous Persian conquest in 490 BC.

FENNEL ~ *continued*

Parts used: Seeds
Specific uses: CONJUNCTIVITIS, COLIC, COUGHS (a mild expectorant) INDIGESTION, FLATULENCE, DIGESTIVE AID

Traditional uses and general information: The essential oil is strongly antibacterial and has been shown to be antispasmodic (muscle relaxing). It is also carminative (easing griping and flatulence). Fennel is used to promote and increase milk flow during breast feeding.

Methods of use and dosage: An infusion made with 1 or 2 tsp of crushed seeds or a fennel teabag in a cup of hot water. Take 3 times daily. A decoction made with 1 or 2 tsp of bruised seeds in a cup of cold water. Take 3 times daily.

The cooled infusion may be used as an eye wash for sore eyes and conjunctivitis. Be sure to strain and filter the liquid carefully.

FENUGREEK ~

Trigonella foenum-graecum

This plant is cultivated in many parts of the world and the seeds used as a 'spice' in cooking.

Part used: Seed
Specific uses: DIGESTIVE AID, NUTRITIVE FOOD, POST GASTROENTERITIS (calms and soothes the digestive tract)

Traditional uses and general information: Traditionally, this herb was used in India to assist lactation in nursing mothers. The Chinese have used Fenugreek to control menopausal sweats ('hot flushes'). In the past it was taken to control blood sugar levels. Latest scientific research indicates that it has a cholesterol lowering effect in people with high cholesterol levels.

Methods of use and dosage: An infusion made with 1 tsp of crushed seeds in a cup of boiling water.

A decoction made with 1 tsp of the bruised seeds in a cup of boiling water. Take the decoction or infusion 3 times daily. 1 tsp of crushed or bruised fennel seeds can be added to make it more palatable.

Tablets and capsules as directed by the manufacturer.

As the seeds are rather bitter, it may be preferable to take them in tablet or capsule form. To obtain the full benefit of the constituents it requires the whole seed to be taken.

FENUGREEK ~ *continued*
Precautions: Not to be used during pregnancy.

FEVERFEW ~
Tanacetum parthenium

Feverfew is a corruption of the latin word 'febrifugia' indicating the plant's former use as a fever reducing medicine.

> *Part used:* Leaves and flowers
> *Specific uses:* MIGRAINE, ARTHRITIS

Traditional uses and general information: Feverfew is commonly used for headaches, migraines and arthritis. Its primary importance in the past was in female complaints, including the regulation of the menstrual cycle and the relief of menstrual pain.

The leaves and flowers may be applied as a poultice to boils and swellings.

Recently, clinical trials have been carried out on the effect of feverfew on migraine. At Kings College, London, some three hundred people were given the fresh leaves over an extended period. 70% of those tested, claimed that their migraines were less painful or less frequent or both, although the remaining 30% gained no apparent relief.

Rosemarinic acid (a compound in feverfew) has an anti–viral action.

Methods of use and dosage: One large or two small leaves (fresh) daily – try with other fillings in a sandwich.
Feverfew essence as directed by the manufacturer.
Tablets and capsules, as directed by the manufacturer.

Precautions: Feverfew may occasionally cause soreness of the mouth or tongue and in some people, dermatitis (or skin rash). Avoid its use in pregnancy, or in children under 6 years of age.

GARLIC ~
Allium sativum

Garlic is a well known culinary herb with medicinal properties which have been recognised for thousands of years. It was noted for its ability to promote strength and endurance. Egyptian labourers building the pyramids took garlic as did the Roman soldiers to increase stamina on long marches.

GARLIC ~ *continued*

Part used: Bulb
Specific uses: COLDS, COUGHS, INFLUENZA,
RESPIRATORY CATARRH, SINUSITIS,
STOMACH UPSETS

Traditional uses and general information: Its primary use today is in the treatment of colds, coughs, influenza, catarrh and other infective conditions. For those prone to recurrent colds etc, it may be used as a preventive measure.

Garlic appears to have the effect of lowering blood cholesterol levels. Externally, it can be applied to wounds for its antiseptic qualities. The Chinese use it to treat indigestion, diarrhoea and whooping cough amongst other things.

Scientific tests on fresh garlic show it to have anti-bacterial and anti-fungal actions, e.g. it was effective against different species of candida (thrush). Aged garlic extracts were found to have a stimulating effect upon the body's immune system – hence its usefulness as a prophylactic in relation to recurrent colds etc.

Methods of use and dosage: Take one clove of raw garlic, crushed or minced, several times daily, e.g. added to salad.

Tablets and capsules as directed by the manufacturer.

GINGER ~
Zingiber officinale

A widely used spice, ginger is a native of the tropical parts of Asia where it has been used in food for centuries to help ward off disease and improve digestion.

Part used: Root
Specific uses: DIGESTIVE AID, INDIGESTION, FLATULENCE
AND COLIC, COLDS (see Recipe No. 8), NAUSEA,
TRAVEL SICKNESS, MENSTRUAL PAIN,
BRUISES, CIRCULATORY STIMULANT

Traditional uses and general information: Scientific research has shown ginger to be powerful in the prevention of nausea and vomiting due to motion sickness. It also indicates some antibacterial properties as well as a mild fever reducing action. It has been postulated that ginger alleviates migraines if taken as a preventative measure.

GINGER ~ *continued*
Methods of use and dosage: A decoction made with ½ tsp of the dried root.
Take decoction twice daily or as required.
Tablets and capsules as directed by the manufacturer.

Precautions: Excessive consumption of ginger may cause irritation of the
digestive tract, if irritation occurs reduce the amount used.

GINKGO ~
Ginkgo biloba
Also known as the Maidenhair-Tree. It was traditionally grown in
Japanese temple gardens.

> *Parts used:* Leaves
> *Specific use:* CIRCULATORY STIMULANT

Traditional uses and general information: It is associated with disorders
affecting elderly people, e.g. degenerative mental health, lack of
circulation, short term memory loss, inability to concentrate, dizzy spells
and vertigo, hearing difficulties (tinnitus), headaches and depression.

Many clinical studies have been carried out on ginkgo. In one trial, (using
double blind and cross over method) ginkgo administered to elderly
patients suffering from lack of concentration, lack of vigilance and
impaired mental performance gave a marked improvement in all patients.

Another trial involved 112 geriatric patients. With those showing
symptoms of cerebral insufficiency (reduced blood flow to brain) there
was a significant improvement in short term memory loss, headaches,
tinnitus and vertigo.

Methods of use and dosage: Tablets and capsules as directed by the manufacturer.

Precautions: Not suitable for children.

GINSENG ~
Panax ginseng
The oriental ginseng is a member of the ivy family and is cultivated in
China, Korea and Japan.

GINSENG ~ *continued*
Parts used: Roots
Specific uses: STRESS RELIEF, MILD DEPRESSION,
TIREDNESS, EXAMINATION NERVES,
SEXUAL INADEQUACY

Traditional uses and general information: Ginseng has been used to combat mental and physical weakness following illness and in old age. The root has been taken by soldiers and cosmonauts to improve alertness and delay fatigue. The ability to cope with stress is increased and it has the prophylactic effect of raising immunity to coughs, colds and other respiratory tract infections. Adaptogenic qualities (i.e. balancing effect on bodily functions) are also reported, e.g. it has both sedative and stimulant effects on the central nervous system thus promoting health.

Methods of use and dosage: Chew the root or tablets in quantities specified by the manufacturer. Best taken mid-morning on an empty stomach.

Precautions: Although generally safe for short term use (3-4 weeks) some adverse side effects have been reported when it is consumed to excess.
Not suitable for children.

GOLDEN SEAL ~
Hydrastis canadensis

A potent plant, golden seal contains the important alkaloids – hydrastine and berberine. It is available for home use in tablet form providing a controlled unit dose. The plant is a potent medicine and should be carefully used preferably under supervision of a medical herbalist.

Part used: Root
Specific uses: CATARRH (especially of the upper respiratory tract),
INDIGESTION & HEARTBURN, APPETITE
ENHANCER, CYSTITIS, GASTRITIS,
ENTERITIS, SORE THROAT,
HAEMORRHOIDS

Traditional uses and general information: The North American Indians used this herb to treat painful menstruation. It is used in the treatment of coughs, promoting expectoration and is taken to alleviate menopausal night sweats (hot flushes).

GOLDEN SEAL ~ *continued*
Methods of use and dosage: Tablets and capsules as directed by the manufacturer.

As a gargle to soothe a sore throat, crush 2-3 tablets, stir into a wine glassful of warm water and gargle 2 or 3 times daily.

Precautions: Avoid use during pregnancy and breast feeding.

Not suitable for children.

HAWTHORN ~
Crataegus oxyacanthoides
Crataegus monogyna
Hawthorn is a hardy hedge plant having white or pink flowers in May and red berries in the Autumn.

> *Parts used:* Fruit, flowers and leaves
> *Specific use:* POOR CIRCULATION

Traditional uses and general information: Hawthorn is primarily used as a circulatory remedy and is often taken as a heart tonic.

The flowers and fruits have been taken for sore throats. In France the blossoms are used to treat nervous disorders.

Methods of use and dosage: An infusion made with 1-2 tsp of the dried flowers, leaves or fruit in a cup of boiling water. Take 3 times daily.

Tablets and capsules, as directed by the manufacturer.

Precautions: Not suitable for children.

HELONIAS ~
Chamaelirium luteum
Helonias is also known as 'False Unicorn Root' or 'Blazing Star Root' and is a native of North America.

> *Part used:* Root
> *Specific use:* PREMENSTRUAL SYNDROME, MENOPAUSE

Traditional uses and general information: Primarily used for its hormonal action, helonias acts as a tonic to the female reproductive system and can help in the maintenance of normal fluid balance. It has also been used to treat infertility and menopausal symptoms.

HELONIAS ~ *continued*
Combine with relaxants in the treatment of menstrual migraine.

Methods of use and dosage: A decoction made with 1–2 tsp of helonias root to a cup of cold water. Take 3 times daily.

Tablets and capsules as directed by the manufacturer.

Precautions: Not suitable for children or during pregnancy.

HOPS ~
Humutus lupulus

Hops belong to the same 'family' as nettles. For many centuries hops have been used in beer making. Prior to this popular drinks were 'ale' or 'mead' which was fermented honey or barley flavoured with certain herbs, e.g. ground ivy, yarrow, marjoram .

> *Parts used:* The female hop (Strobiles)
> *Specific uses:* APPETITE ENHANCER, INSOMNIA, NERVOUS STOMACH UPSETS, NERVOUS TENSION, ANXIETY, IRRITABLE BOWEL, NERVOUS DIARRHOEA

Traditional uses and general information: Hops have a mild sedative effect on the central nervous system and have long been used to treat excitability, restlessness and insomnia. A pillow filled with hops is one way in which they are used to induce sleep.

Hops can be taken for problems of the digestive tract caused by tension, e.g. nervous diarrhoea.

Applied externally it has been used to treat wounds and sores because of its antiseptic qualities.

Methods of use and dosage: An infusion made with 1 tsp of the dried strobiles in a cup of water. Take 3 times daily.

Tablets and capsules as directed by the manufacturer.

Precautions: Not suitable for children or adults suffering from depression.

KELP ~
Fucus vesiculosus

Kelp is a seaweed growing along the coast, from the Atlantic to the Baltic Oceans.

KELP ~ *continued*
Parts used: Whole plant
Specific use: NUTRITIONAL FOOD

Traditional uses and general information: Kelp is an excellent nutritional food due to its vitamin and mineral content. It is particularly high in calcium and iron but also contains a wide range of other minerals in trace amounts. It contains iodine which is necessary for proper thyroid function. (The Thyroid gland is the governing gland for the body's metabolism.)

Traditionally, it has been used to treat obesity and to relieve rheumatic pains.

N.B. Iodine was added to table salt to correct the nutritional deficiencies occurring in some parts of the country, where there was increased incidence of thyroid gland dysfunction. Therefore for those on a salt restricted diet kelp may form an excellent natural source of the necessary iodine.

Methods of use and dosage: An infusion made with 1-2 tsps of the dried plant. Take 3 times daily.

Tablets and capsules as directed by the manufacturer.

LAVENDER ~
Lavendula officinalis

A very well known herb, indigenous to Mediterranean countries, lavender has been grown extensively in Britain in the past. Now, however, it is found in only a few locations although it is still widely cultivated in France and elsewhere on the Continent. The name 'lavender' is derived from the latin 'lavandus' meaning 'to be washed'. The Romans were known to take lavender baths to alleviate minor skin diseases.

Parts used: (i) Flowers in herbal preparations
(ii) An essential oil extracted from the flowers (see below)
Specific uses: STRESS RELIEF, MILD DEPRESSION, INDIGESTION, FLATULENCE, COLIC, STRESS/ TENSION HEADACHES

Traditional uses and general information: This herb can be used as a tonic to the nervous system and is especially relevant where depression is combined with digestive problems.

LAVENDER ~ *continued*

A lavender bag placed amongst clothing has been used for generations to inhibit moths and give the clothes a pleasant aroma.

Methods of use and dosage: An infusion made with 1 tsp of the herb. Take 3 times daily.

Apply a lotion to eczema + itchy skin.

LAVENDER OIL ~

Used in a wide range of perfumery and cosmetic preparations, lavender oil is noted for its fresh-sweet, herbal-floral fragrance. The oil yield from lavender is 0.5–2.1%.

> *Specific uses:* MINOR BURNS, HEADACHES (due to stress, tension and influenza), STRESS RELIEF, INFLAMMATORY SKIN CONDITIONS, SORE AND CHAPPED HANDS (soothing and healing)

Methods of use and dosage: As a relaxant: 4–5 drops in the bath, 2–3 drops mixed with 5ml vegetable oil massaged below the nose and on the temples, avoiding area around the eyes.

For mild burns; immediately apply a few drops of neat oil.

For sore chapped hands and inflammatory skin conditions: mix 5–6 drops in 5ml vegetable oil or a dessert spoonful of vegetable margarine, gently massage into the skin. Because of the greasy properties, it is helpful to wear cotton gloves for a time.

For headaches see formula no. 4, sinusitis see Recipe No. 3

Precautions: Do not use internally without professional advice. If signs of skin irritation appear discontinue use.

LEMON BALM~

Melissa officinalis

The essential oil is partly responsible for the 'lemony' aroma released when leaves are bruised. In the past, branches of lemon balm were strewn over the floor in order to freshen the room

Lemon balm was said to ensure longevity.

LEMON BALM ~ *continued*
Parts used: Leaves
Specific uses: INFLUENZA, HEADACHES, COLDS, STRESS
RELIEF, INSOMNIA, COLD SORES

Traditional uses and general information: Lemon balm is a relaxant herb. It was used in France as a tonic and for headaches or tiredness. It is reported that the tea has anti-viral properties, it is effective in the treatment of cold sores (herpes simplex) and has an antibacterial action similar to that of rosemary. The oil yield from the plant is very low, less than 0.1%. It is a gentle but effective remedy especially suitable for children.

Methods of use and dosage: An infusion made with 1-2 tsps of the dried leaves in a cup of warm water. (Ensure the cup is covered while leaves infusing). Take 2-3 times daily.

For cold sores: Apply a compress to the affected area.

For a relaxing bath: Add a few sprigs of the *fresh* plant to the bath water. A few rose petals add extra effect.

LIQUORICE ~
Glycyrrhiza glabra

The name 'glycyrrhiza' or 'sweet root' comes from the Greek 'glukas' (sweet) and 'rhiza' (root). It has been widely cultivated for the pharmaceutical, food and tobacco industries.

Part used: Root
Specific uses: INDIGESTION, HEARTBURN, COUGHS,
GASTRITIS

Traditional uses and general information: Liquorice is included in cough mixtures as a soothing expectorant. In some herbal (and indeed pharmaceutical) preparations, liquorice is added for its sweetness to mask strong or bitter flavours of other herbs or drugs. It has a mild laxative action and components of the root have been shown to have anti-arthritic activity.

Methods of use and dosage: A decoction made with ½-1 tsp of the root to a cup of cold water. Take 3 times daily.

Tablets and capsules, as directed by the manufacturer.

Precautions: Excessive consumption of liquorice has been known to cause a wide range of systemic upsets, including increased blood pressure, fluid retention, headaches and fatigue. However the body returns to normal with no apparent lasting effects when consumption of liquorice ceases.

LIME BLOSSOM ~
Tilia europea

The European lime tree is decorative and sweetly scented and is grown in parks and gardens lining many avenues and driveways.

> *Part used:* Flowers
> *Specific uses:* STRESS RELIEF, COLDS and INFLUENZA, CONSTIPATION (caused by tension)

Traditional uses and general information: Lime blossom is taken as a tisane in France and Germany. In France, it is specifically taken after meals to assist digestion and to promote sleep.

Medical herbalists use lime blossom in conjunction with other plant remedies to treat heart and circulatory conditions. It also provides children with a gentle remedy for nervous tension.

Methods of use and dosage: An infusion made with 1-2 tsp of lime blossom in a cup of hot water. Take 3 to 4 times daily.

Tablets and capsules as directed by the manufacturer.

MARIGOLD ~
Calendula officinalis

The Romans used marigold petals as a substitute for saffron due to the beautiful bright orange colour of the marigold flower.

> *Parts used:* Petals or whole flowers
> *Specific uses:* BURNS AND WOUNDS (minor), BOILS, BRUISES, TO IMPROVE CIRCULATION, HAEMORRHOIDS, CONJUNCTIVITIS

Traditional uses and general information: The plant is used for a wide variety of conditions. According to W. Hale White M.D., F.R.C.P. Lecturer on Medicine at Guy's Hospital (1901), when applied to ulcers it 'decreases odour, cleans surfaces, relieves pain and promotes repair'. It has also been used to reduce fever due to its ability to induce sweating. Marigold may be included in mouth washes. The ointment may be applied to eczema, nappy rashes and scalds. Marigold cream can be used for sunburn. It has a slight sedative action and was taken for painful periods and stomach cramps.

Methods of use and dosage: An infusion made with 1-2 tsp of dried flowers in a cup of boiling water. Take 3 times daily. Use the infusion as a mouth wash for mouth ulcers.

MARIGOLD ~ *continued*

Apply as a lotion to burns, wounds and bruises. Apply regularly. Also use the cooled lotion as an eye wash for conjunctivitis – ensuring it is well strained and filtered to remove all particles from the liquid.

Tablets and capsules as directed by the manufacturer.

MOTHERWORT ~
Leonurus cardiaca

The Japanese believed Motherwort to have properties which promote longevity. The plant is a herb native to Europe and was introduced to Britain centuries ago.

> *Parts used:* Aerial parts
> *Specific uses:* ANXIETY, MENOPAUSAL HOT FLUSHES, HEART TONIC, NERVOUS PALPITATIONS

Traditional uses and general information: Motherwort is used for anxiety conditions related to the female reproductive system. As its name 'cardiaca' suggests it is used for the cardio-vascular system. It has also been used in the treatment of hysteria.

Methods of use and dosage: An infusion made with 1-2 tsp of dried herb. Take 3 times daily.

Tablets and capsules as directed by the manufacturer.

Precautions: Not to be taken during pregnancy.

NETTLES ~
Urtica dioica

Contrary to popular opinion, the nettle is not simply a garden menace but has important medicinal properties.

> *Parts used:* Aerial parts
> *Specific uses:* NUTRITIONAL FOOD, ECZEMA, MILD DIARRHOEA, ARTHRITIS, MINOR WOUNDS AND GRAZES

NETTLES ~ *continued*

Traditional uses and general information: In the past, the tough stem fibres of the nettle were used to make cloth. The plant was also included in the diet as a good source of vitamins and minerals, the young leaves being cooked as a vegetable or made into soup. In fact, Hippocrates lists the nettle under 'vegetable foods'. The nettle is used to treat arthritis and gout, to promote milk flow, to staunch bleeding wounds and as a hair tonic to stimulate hair growth.

Methods of use and dosage: An infusion made with 1-2 tsp of the dried leaves in a cup of hot water. Take 3 times daily. Use a lotion for minor wounds and grazes.

For mild dandruff or as a hair tonic make a decoction with 4 tbsp of nettle leaves to ½l of water. Allow to cool then massage into hair and scalp.

Tablet and capsules as directed by the manufacturer.

PASSION FLOWER ~

Passiflora incarnata

The 'passion fruit' available from supermarkets belongs to the same family as the passion flower used in herbal medicine. The fruit from the latter species, however, is not edible!

> *Parts used:* Aerial parts
> *Specific uses:* INSOMNIA, HEADACHES (caused by stress)

Traditional uses and general information: The passion flower has a mild sedative action on the central nervous system as well as having muscle-relaxing and pain relieving properties. It has been used to combat restlessness, hysteria, nervous tension, neuralgia and shingles.

Methods of use and dosage: An infusion made with 1 tsp of dried herb in a cup of boiling water. Take twice a day or as required. In the treatment of insomnia take shortly before going to bed.

Tablets and capsules as directed by the manufacturer.

Precautions: Not suitable for children under 5 years old.

PEPPERMINT ~

Mentha piperita

Peppermint is another widely-used herb, principally in conditions associated with the gastro-intestinal tract (digestive tract).

43

PEPPERMINT ~ *continued*

English peppermint; a variety known as 'Mitcham' was, in the past, considered to be the finest in the world and is still available in some parts of the country.

Parts used: (i) Leaf in herbal preparations
(ii) An essential oil distilled from the leaves used in Aromatherapy and the food industry

Specific uses: INTESTINAL COLIC, IRRITABLE BOWEL, NAUSEA, TRAVEL SICKNESS, TO CALM STOMACH AFTER VOMITTING, INDIGESTION, FLATULENCE (it increases the release of bile from the gall bladder and stimulates the liver in addition to its calming action), COLDS, INFLUENZA, DIARRHOEA, STRESS HEADACHES, INSOMNIA, SORE THROATS

Traditional uses and general information: It has been scientifically proven that the consumption of peppermint tea has two distinct effects. Initially, it causes excitation of the central nervous system due to the effect on the senses of the peppermint oil followed by a *sedative* effect from the tea. This makes it particularly useful as a pre-bedtime drink. Taken an hour before settling down, it helps to promote healthy sleep.

Methods of use and dosage: An infusion made with 1-2 tsps of peppermint or a peppermint teabag in a cup of hot water. Take the infusion 3-4 times daily. For sedative effect leave the pot uncovered while infusing to allow the essential oil to evaporate.

Use an infusion as a gargle for a sore throat. It is a good idea to combine peppermint with other herbs. See 'Plants for Specific Ailments' page 14.

In the bath for day time use: It has been found that a small quantity (2 teabags or tsps tied in a muslin bag) in the bath will act as a gentle stimulant giving a refreshing wakefulness due to inhalation of the volatile essential oil evaporating from the hot water, this excites the nervous system as mentioned above.

PEPPERMINT OIL ~

This is a very potent form of administration and should be used sparingly and only short term; i.e. 2-3 days.

PEPPERMINT OIL ~ *continued*
Specific uses: SINUSITIS (see Formula No. 3), HEADACHES (see Formula No. 4), NAUSEA, FOOD POISONING (mild), UPSET STOMACH, TRAVEL SICKNESS

Methods of use and dosage: 1 drop of essential oil on a lump of sugar or on a teasp of sugar.

Travel sickness: Take 1 drop before travelling. If nausea persists, take a further 1 drop after one hour.

Nausea, upset stomach, mild food poisoning: Take 1 drop up to a maximum of 3 times daily. Use for no more than 2-3 days.

For children under 12 use strong peppermint sweets.

For sinusitis see Recipe No. 3. For headaches see Recipe No. 4. Gastritis/oesophagitis see Recipe No. 5. For coughs see Recipe No. 10.

Precautions: Excessive use can cause damage to the delicate mucous membrane lining the mouth and digestive tract.

In cases of extreme sensitivity its use may cause an acquired allergic skin reaction. If this should occur, discontinue its use.

Do not apply directly to the skin.

Avoid during pregnancy.

PULSATILLA ~
Anenome pulsatilla

Pulsatilla is also known as meadow anenome or pasque flower. In Great Britain this plant is a protected species when growing in the wild.

Parts used: Aerial parts
Specific uses: HEADACHES or MIGRAINE (caused or aggravated by stress), PREMENSTRUAL TENSION

Traditional uses and general information: Pulsatilla has relaxant properties which makes it helpful for insomnia. It is usefully given in painful and inflamed conditions of the reproductive tract, e g. menstrual pain (especially when there is a light flow) and for skin problems, e.g. boils and acne.

Methods of use and dosage: An infusion of ¼-1 tsp of dried pulsatilla in a cup of boiling water. Take 3 times daily or as required.

PULSATILLA ~ *continued*
Tablets and capsules as directed by the manufacturer.

Precaution: The fresh plant must not be used as it is poisonous. This does not apply to the plant in its dry state. Not suitable for children.

RED CLOVER~
Trifolium pratense

Common in pastures and meadows. This plant is named 'trifolium' because of its three-lobed leaves. It has been widely cultivated as animal fodder and with other grasses produces the finest hay.

> *Parts used:* Flower heads
> *Specific uses:* ECZEMA

Traditional uses and general information: It is mainly used as a cleansing remedy for skin conditions. Also used for coughs due to its expectorant action and in the past has been taken for whooping cough. Externally, it may be applied to sores and ulcers. It is a good remedy for childhood eczema.

Methods of use and dosage: An infusion made with 1-2 tsps of dried red clover in a cup of boiling water. Take 3 times daily.

Tablets and capsules as directed by the manufacturer.

RED SAGE ~
Salvia officinalis

An Arabian proverb translates, 'how can a man die who grows sage in his garden'.

> *Parts used:* Leaves
> *Specific uses:* SORE THROATS, LARYNGITIS, GINGIVITIS, MILD FOOD POISONING, RESPIRATORY CATARRH, MOUTH ULCERS (apthous ulcers), MILD DIARRHOEA, COLDS AND FLU, TONSILLITIS, MENOPAUSAL HOT FLUSHES

Traditional uses and general information: Red sage has been used to inhibit night sweats, to treat indigestion and nervous headaches, for calming nerves and soothing sore throats. Greek women rubbed their teeth with sage leaves. Sage has proved useful when taken to dry up milk flow when weaning.

RED SAGE ~ *continued*

Methods of use and dosage: An infusion made with ½-1 tsp of sage in a cup of hot water. Take 3 times daily.

Use an infusion as a mouth wash for sore throats, gingivitis, laryngitis and mouth ulcers (see Recipe No. 1 page 58).

Tablets and capsules as directed by the manufacturer.

Precautions: Avoid internal use during pregnancy and while breast feeding.

ROSEMARY ~
Rosmarinus officinalis

This plant was sacred to Venus and was believed to give eternal youth. Furthermore, Greek students took it to improve their memory!

> *Parts used:* Leaves and twigs
> *Specific uses:* TIREDNESS (mental and physical), STRESS HEADACHES, INDIGESTION with FLATULENCE and COLIC (the essential oil has an antispasmodic action – the plant extract increases bile flow)

Traditional uses and general information: Rosemary has been used for longevity, to improve the memory and, externally, to stimulate the hair follicles and prevent premature baldness. A simple infusion of dried rosemary as a hairwash will help to improve the lustre of dark hair (see Recipe No. 7). The oil is massaged into the scalp for dandruff and other scaly conditions of the scalp. Rosemary has been investigated for its anti-viral action and the oil is strongly antibacterial. It may ease neuralgia, sciatica and muscular pain. (Use the oil diluted in vegetable oil as a rub.)

Methods of use and dosage: An infusion made with 1 tsp of dried rosemary. Take 3 times daily.

Scalp application: 6-7 drops of rosemary oil mixed into 5ml of vegetable oil (preferably jojoba). Massage into the scalp as required. Home-made rosemary oil may be used in its place (see below).

For baths: Add a few sprigs of dried rosemary to warm bath water. (It is advised not to use fresh rosemary as this is too resinous.)

For a homemade rosemary oil: Add a couple of sprigs of rosemary to sunflower or olive oil (ensuring all the material is immersed in the oil). Leave in a sunny position for a few weeks. Remove the sprigs and use the delicately flavoured oil in food, on the skin or as a bath oil.

N.B. Do not use commercial essential oil of rosemary internally.

SLIPPERY ELM ~
Ulmus fulva

Slippery elm is a tree which grows in the United States and Canada. In the spring the bark is stripped and the outer cortex removed. The inner bark has the medicinal properties.

> *Part used:* Inner bark
> *Specific uses:* POST GASTRO-ENTERITIS, OESOPHAGITIS, MINOR STOMACH UPSETS, INDIGESTION and HEARTBURN, NUTRITIONAL FOOD, MINOR WOUNDS, BOILS

Traditional uses and general information: Slippery elm is calming and soothing to the digestive tract and is, therefore, useful in treating most inflammatory conditions. As a nutritional food it is easily digested and may be taken during convalescence. Slippery elm is a suitable remedy for most age groups.

Methods of use and dosage: Add a cup of hot water or milk gradually to 1-2 tsps of slippery elm powder stirring continually, (it easily forms lumps). Drink immediately. Take 3 times daily approximately ½ hour before meals.

Poultice: For minor wounds and boils (see methods of preparation).

Tablets and capsules as directed by the manufacturer.

ST JOHN'S WORT ~
Hypericum perforatum

St John's Wort's bright yellow flowers yield a red oil which has been used since the middle ages. It was applied to wounds of the Crusader Knights.

> *Parts used:* Aerial parts
> *Specific uses:* ANXIETY, MENOPAUSAL TENSION, MINOR BURNS, NEURALGIA

Traditional uses and general information: A plant well known for its ability to heal wounds and sores. St John's wort is helpful in healing damaged nerves and in the treatment of neuralgia and sciatica. This herb has also found a place in the treatment of colds, coughs and catarrh. Extracts have been found to have broad spectrum anti-bacterial properties. Externally applied, the oil is useful not only in wound healing and sunburn but also for neuralgia and sciatica. Throughout Europe, St John's wort is taken as a relaxant. In Italy the oil is used externally on cold sores (Herpes simplex). One clinical study showed that in the treatment of anxiety it was several weeks before the full benefits became apparent.

ST JOHN'S WORT ~ *continued*

Methods of use and dosage: An infusion made with 1-2 tsps of the dried herb. Take 3 times daily.

Tablets and capsules as directed by the manufacturer.

Lotion: For minor wounds, mild burns and bruises.

The oil: Applied to cold sores, neuralgia, sciatica, fibrositis. See Recipe No. 9.

Precautions: St John's wort can occasionally cause photosensitivity, therefore avoid long periods of exposure to strong sunlight when using this plant. Do not apply to areas of skin where long exposure is unavoidable.

THYME ~
Thymus vulgaris

A plant native to the Mediterranean region and Asia Minor, but also a common garden plant in Great Britain. It has been used by past generations to overcome shyness.

> Parts used: Leaves and flowering tops
> Specific uses: COUGHS, NERVOUS COUGHS, SORE
> THROATS, GINGIVITIS, LARYNGITIS,
> INDIGESTION, FLATULENCE, COLIC,
> CYSTITIS, MILD DIARRHOEA, GASTRO~
> ENTERITIS, MILD FOOD POISONING, MINOR
> WOUNDS/GRAZES

Traditional uses and general information: The ancient Assyrian herbal quotes thyme for treatment of lung and stomach complaints. The oil is known to be strongly anti-bacterial and anti-fungal. Thyme has been used to loosen catarrh in the respiratory tract. The hot infusion is taken to promote sweating and has been used to increase appetite.

Methods of use and dosage: An infusion made with 1 tsp of dried thyme. Take 3 times daily.

Use an infusion as a gargle for sore throats, gingivitis, laryngitis. Apply the lotion externally for minor wounds and grazes.

UVA URSI ~
Arctostaphylos uva-ursi

Uva Ursi is also known as bearberry. Bears are supposedly attracted to the berries of some species.

Parts used: Leaves
Specific uses: CYSTITIS, URETHRITIS

Traditional uses and general information: Uva ursi is used for urinary tract infections because of its diuretic and antiseptic properties. A major therapeutic constituent arbutin changes within the body to hydro-quinone which is anti-microbial.

Methods of use and dosage: An infusion made with 1-2 tsp of the dried leaves in a cup of boiling water. Take 3 times daily.

Tablets and capsules, as directed by the manufacturer.

Precautions: Not suitable for children.

VALERIAN ~
Valeriana officinalis

The name Valerian is believed to be derived from the latin word 'valere', meaning to be in good health.

Parts used: Roots
Specific uses: EXCITABILITY, EXAMINATION NERVES,
                  HEADACHES, INSOMNIA, MENSTRUAL PAIN,
                  STRESS RELIEF, ECZEMA

Traditional uses and general information: Valerian has been widely used in the treatment of anxiety, over-excitability and nervous tension. It is taken for insomnia where it can help to improve the quality of sleep.

A lotion of valerian is sometimes applied to eczema.

Scientific research has shown that valerian has sedative, relaxant and anti-spasmodic (muscle relaxing) qualities.

Methods of use and dosage: A decoction made with 1 tsp of the dried root in a cup of cold water. Take 3 times daily or as required.

Tablets and capsules as directed by the manufacturer.

VITEX ~
Vitex agnus castus

Vitex agnus castus is also known as chasteberry or monks pepper, but was first used by the vestal virgins in the temples of ancient Greece.

Part used: Fruit
Specific uses: PRE-MENSTRUAL SYNDROME, MENOPAUSAL HOT FLUSHES

Traditional uses and general information: The Egyptians used bandages with vitex seeds, ground barley and red ochre to reduce swellings, mixed vitex with water to strengthen the teeth and used it internally with other ingredients to treat constipation. In the past, monks took agnus-castus as an aphrodisiac hence its name chasteberry. Modern medical herbalists use it to normalise the female sex hormones and anterior pituitary function, especially with regard to progesterone levels. (The pituitary is a small gland which plays an important role in regulating the body's hormone levels.) It is also given to stimulate milk flow.

Antibacterial properties have definitely been attributed to vitex agnus castus leaves. Recent studies on vitex fruit in treatment of pre-menstrual syndrome indicate that it had the greatest effect on water retention and breast tenderness.

Methods of use and dosage: An infusion made with 1 tsp of the crushed berries in a cup of boiling water. Take 3 times daily.

Tablets and capsules as directed by the manufacturer.

Precautions: Not suitable for children.

WILD YAM ~
Dioscorea villosa

The roots have been used as food for generations; they have a high starch content. Certain species of wild yams provide essential starting material for the manufacture of contraceptive pills.

Part used: Root
Specific uses: RHEUMATOID ARTHRITIS, INTESTINAL COLIC

WILD YAM ~ *continued*

Traditional uses and general information: The wild yam is used for its anti-inflammatory and anti-spasmodic actions due to the presence of naturally occurring steroidal glycosides. Wild yam was the subject of research when the steroidal glycosides were identified. These were shown to be related to steroids produced in the human body.

Methods of use and dosage: As a decoction, 1-2 tsps of dried root in a cup of cold water. Take 3 times daily.

Tablets and capsules as directed by the manufacturer.

Precautions: Not suitable for children.

5 | Pregnancy

The current view is that non-essential medication should be avoided during pregnancy. However a few plants may be safely used for short periods, i.e. 2-3 weeks, but always seek medical advice prior to their use.

For definition of symbols, e.g. d c/t refer to key symbols page 14.

For tips on purchase, gathering, storage and preparation 'Making the Most of Plants' page 11.

RASPBERRY LEAF TEA – May be taken during the last 3 months of pregnancy to strengthen and tone the muscle tissue of the womb. Traditionally, it has been found effective in easing labour.

Methods of use and dosage: Make an infusion with 1-2 tsp of the dried herb in a cupful of boiling water. Take this infusion 2-3 times daily.

Tablets and capsules as directed by the manufacturers.

CONSTIPATION – A common problem of pregnancy. It is best controlled by diet.

Plants used: DANDELION ROOT (d c/t), RAISINS (f), SLIPPERY ELM (fi t). If 'overtone constipation' (constipation caused by tension) use relaxants.

MILK FLOW – To increase: Fennel (i d), Fenugreek (f i/d c/t), Nettle (i f).
  – To dry up when weaning: Sage (i).
    N.B. Do not take sage at any other time during pregnancy or breast feeding.

MORNING SICKNESS – Crystalline ginger (f) nibble small quantities, cinnamon and ginger (i), peppermint (i).

Cinnamon and ginger tea: Make an infusion made with ½ tsp of cinnamon powder and a pinch of dried powdered ginger in a cup of hot water. Add honey to taste and sip small quantities as required.

RELAXANTS – Chamomile (i), lemon balm (i), lavender oil (a) (see lavender herb), lime blossom (i), valerian (d c/t).

SORE NIPPLES – Chamomile teabags (i).

Infuse for a few minutes. Allow to cool to comfortable temperature and apply teabag over nipple area to soothe and subdue inflammation.

Leave until completely cool.

Chamomile or marigold cream can also be used. These are commercially available.

Precautions: Avoid the internal use of all other plants and oils mentioned in this book except under professional guidance.

BABIES – up to 1 year

COLIC – Peppermint (i), fennel (crushed) (i), chamomile (i).

NAPPY RASH – Chamomile (l), marigold (l), lavender (l). Comfrey ointment, which is commercially available.

TO AID SLEEP – Chamomile (i), lemon balm (i), lime blossom (i).

Methods of use and dosage: Infusions. 1 teabag or 1 tsp of herb to 100ml of hot water makes 3 doses. Take one dose per day. When treating colic the dose need not be given all at once. To aid sleep give the full dose just before settling down.

6 | Warnings and Cautions

Are herbs safe?

It is not uncommon to hear members of the scientific and medical professions issuing warnings of the dangers of herbal preparations. The following information is provided to put these claims into perspective.

There are toxic herbs but the vast majority are not available to the general public. Of the handful of herbs known to contain potentially hazardous compounds, it is usually found that vast consumption, far in excess of normal, is required to constitute a danger; in many cases once the over-consumption has ceased the body returns to normal. An example is liquorice, where over-consumption can lead to severe physiological disturbances, yet in reported cases where this has occurred it is noteworthy that, once consumption ceased, the symptoms disappeared and the body returned to *normal*. This effect of many natural substances differs greatly from synthetic drugs where overuse can lead to *permanent, irreparable damage* – particularly with medicines bought over the counter, like paracetamol and aspirin.

Solanine poisoning from potatoes is interesting

In *scientific* literature reviews, there are reports of 2000 cases of poisoning from potatoes worldwide including 12 deaths. It is suggested that many cases are unreported as the symptoms are similar to those of mild food poisoning.

The lethal dose of the alkaloid responsible is 3-6mg/kg.

1 mg is the average daily intake from only 300 grams of potatoes.

Early varieties were found to contain levels of alkaloid far in excess of the toxic dose.

It is therefore fortunate that consumption of new potatoes tends to be lower than old.

Despite this, no calls are made to ban potatoes or even make the public aware of the dangers of excessive consumption.

Gathering herbs

1) Correct identification of the plants is essential. Refer to the book list for guides.

2) Do not gather protected species of wild plants from the countryside, or any other plants without the consent of the person on whose land they grow.
3) Remember that plants growing close to the roadside are likely to be polluted.

Self medication

It is inadvisable to undertake self medication using medicinal plants for extended periods, i.e. for longer than 2-3 weeks at a time without a break. If a condition persists beyond a reasonable length of time, consult a medical herbalist or a medical practitioner.

Pregnancy and babies
Refer to specific section, page 53.

Children

Certain plants are not suitable for children. Refer to precautions under individual plants in the 'A-Z of Medicinal Plants'.

Essential oils

1) For exact instructions on the use of essential oils mentioned in this book, refer to the section on 'Making the Most of Plants' and under individual plants in the 'A-Z of Medicinal Plants'.
2) Do NOT administer essential oils to children under five years of age without consulting a medical herbalist or aromatherapist.
3) Avoid eye area and always wash hands after use. If an accident occurs wash the eyes with plenty of cold water and seek medical attention.
4) Keep all essential oils out of the reach of children – especially the pleasant tasting ones! – and take care when using bowls of boiling water for inhalation.

Sensitivity reactions

A sensitivity reaction is different from a toxicity reaction. With sensitisation the body is building up a reaction to a repeatedly used substance. Certain families of plants are more likely to cause sensitivity reactions than others, e.g. those belonging to the compositae family: chamomile, feverfew etc have been known to produce these reactions in a few people. However, with peppermint, a member of the labiate family, there are very few reports of sensitivity.

The likelihood of a sensitivity reaction from gathering fresh plants is substantially greater than when using dried material. If a skin rash develops when gathering fresh plants, wear cotton gloves on all future occasions. It does not necessarily follow that you will have a sensitivity reaction when taking the fresh plant as a tea so experiment with fresh or dry plant material for internal use, (as tea or tablets). If, however, further skin rashes or irritation develop, cease using the plant.

Drug interactions

Most of the plants mentioned in this book are not known to cause adverse reactions when taken in conjunction with other medication. If you are unsure you should check with your general practitioner or a medical herbalist.

7 | Recipes

1. SORE THROAT: GINGIVITIS, LARYNGITIS

Take 3-6 tsps fresh or 1-2 tsps dried chamomile or 2 teabags.
2 sprigs of fresh or 1 tsp dried thyme.
1 tsp of fresh or ½ tsp dried sage.

N.B. If either sage or thyme are not available one can be omitted.

Infuse in a cupful of hot water for 5-10 mins, strain, gargle or swill round the mouth and drink 2-3 times daily.

N.B. Omit 'sage' during pregnancy or breast feeding.

2. FOLLOWING TOOTH EXTRACTION

Make a strong chamomile infusion with 2 teabags, when cool strain and apply to the gums, or use as a mouthwash. One drop of lavender oil can be applied using the tip of a CLEAN finger.

3. SINUSITIS

Inhalation: Use oils of; lavender, pine needle, teatree, or peppermint.
Peppermint is a strong oil use only one drop either alone or within a mixture. Use 2-3 drops of a single oil (other than peppermint) or combine any of the above oils up to a maximum of 6 drops, e.g. lavender 2 drops, peppermint 1 drop, pine needle 2 drops, teatree 1 drop, total 6 drops.

Method
Pour 1-2 litres of boiling water into a bowl.
Add the selected oils to the water and place the head over the bowl.
Cover the head with a towel KEEPING EYES CLOSED.
Breathe normally inhaling the vapour for a few minutes at a time (as comfortable) over a 10 minute period. Repeat 2-3 times a day if required.

Warning
Do not go out into cold air for at least ½ hour after inhalation; the delicate mucous membranes of the nose will be sensitive. Avoid long term and constant use.

4. HEADACHES

Fresh rose petals. Float a few petals in the bath or enclose them in muslin, these petals can also be dried in a sunny position, stored then used as above.

Essential oils: Lavender, 2 drops plus peppermint, 1 drop. Mix with 5ml vegetable oil.

Method

Rub the mixed oils on temple area and below the nose, (keeping well away from the eyes).

Can be repeated several times a day as necessary but avoid constant use.

N.B. Wash fingers after use.

5. GASTRITIS/OESOPHAGITIS

Place one drop of peppermint oil on a slippery elm tablet and take one tablet 3 times daily approximately $\frac{1}{2}$ hour before meals for 1 or 2 days.

6. TO LIGHTEN HAIR COLOUR

Chamomile paste

6 tbsps chamomile flower heads

500ml water

8 tbsps kaolin powder

1 egg yolk

Place flower heads in a coffee grinder or crush with a rolling pin.

Make an infusion by immersing the flower heads in boiling water, leave to stand for 20 minutes.

When cooled, strain off 285ml of liquid.

Stir in the kaolin powder and egg yolk and apply to the hair.

Leave on for 20-50 mins.

Rinse with warm water.

Several applications may be needed to obtain the required lightness of the hair colour.

7. TO DARKEN HAIR COLOUR AND FOR MILD DANDRUFF

Make a decoction using 2 tsp dried rosemary and 2 tsp dried sage to a mugful of water. Allow to cool, strain then massage into the hair and scalp or use as hair rinse.

8. COLDS

1 tsp dried powdered ginger, $\frac{1}{4}$ tsp of cayenne pepper and a pinch of salt (to enable mixing).

Stir together and infuse in a small cup of hot water for 5-10 mins.
Strain, add juice of ½ lime or lemon (for vitamin C content) and swallow immediately.
Can be followed with a glass of cold water.
Take a maximum of twice daily for a few days (if necessary) allowing at least 4 hours between doses.
Do not use if suffering from stomach ulcers.

9. NEURALGIA, SCIATICA ETC

St John's Wort oil: Pick the flowering tops of St John's wort, add them to either olive or sunflower oil in a clear glass container.

Ensure that all the plant material is immersed in the oil.

Place in a sunny position for several weeks until the oil has turned red.

Filter off the oil by squeezing the mixture through a cloth and store in a dark glass bottle in a cool place.

10. EXPECTORANT COUGH MIXTURE

Take 2 sprigs of fresh or 2 tsps of dried thyme and 1½ tsps of fresh or ½ tsp of dried sage to a cup of hot water, add a tsp of honey to the water and allow to infuse for 10-15 mins.
Strain and add the juice of ½ lemon and 1 drop of peppermint oil, mix well. Take this mix sipping, gargling and swallowing.
Use twice a day up to a maximum of 2-3 days.

11. ARTHRITIS

Essential oils: Rosemary 20 drops, juniper 10 drops.
Mix with 20ml of vegetable oil.
Massage the affected joint with a small amount of the mixed oil.

8 | Book List

● PLANT IDENTIFICATION
The Country Life Guide to Edible and Medicinal Plants of Britain and Northern Europe, Edmund Launert
The Macdonald Encyclopaedia of Medicinal Plants

● HISTORY OF PLANT MEDICINE
Green Pharmacy, Barbara Griggs

● PLANT MEDICINE
A Modern Herbal, Mrs Grieves
Healing Plants – A Modern Herbal, William A.R. Thomson M.D.

OTHER BOOKS FROM AMBERWOOD PUBLISHING ARE:

Aromatherapy – A Guide for Home Use by Christine Westwood. All you need to know about essential oils and using them. £1.99.

Aromatherapy – For Stress Management by Christine Westwood. Covering the use of essential oils for everyday stress-related problems. £2.99.

Aromatherapy – For Healthy Legs and Feet by Christine Westwood. A comprehensive guide to the use of essential oils for the treatment of legs and feet, including illustrated massage instructions. £2.99.

Aromatherapy – Simply For You by Marion Del Gaudio Mak. A clear, simple and comprehensive guide to Aromatherapy for beginners. £1.99.

Aromatherapy – A Nurses Guide by Ann Percival SRN. This book draws on the author's medical skills and experience as a qualified aromatherapist to provide the ultimate, safe, lay guide to the natural benefits of Aromatherapy. Including recipes and massage techniques for many medical conditions and a quick reference chart. £2.99.

Aromatherapy – A Nurses Guide for Women by Ann Percival SRN. Building on the success of her first 'Nurses Guide', this book concentrates on women's health for all ages. Including sections on PMT, menopause, infertility, cellulite. Everything a woman needs to know about healthcare using aromatherapy. £2.99.

Aroma Science – The Chemistry & Bioactivity of Essential Oils by Dr Maria Lis-Balchin. With a comprehensive list of the Oils and scientific analysis – a must for all with an interest in the science of Aromatherapy. Includes sections on methodology, the sense of smell and the history of Aromatherapy. £4.99.

Woman Medicine – Vitex Agnus Castus by Simon Mills MA, FNIMH. The wonderful story of the herb that has been used for centuries in the treatment of women's problems. £2.99.

Ancient Medicine – Ginkgo Biloba (New Edition) by Dr Desmond Corrigan BSc(Pharms), MA, Phd, FLS, FPSI. Improved memory, circulation and concentration are associated in this book with medicine from this fascinating tree. £2.99.

Indian Medicine – The Immune System by Dr Desmond Corrigan BSc(Pharms), MA, Phd, FLS, FPSI. An intriguing account of the history and science of the plant called Echinacea and its power to influence the immune system. £2.99.

Herbal Medicine for Sleep & Relaxation by Dr Desmond Corrigan BSc(Pharms), MA, PhD, FLS, FPSI. An expertly written guide to the natural sedatives as an alternative to orthodox drug therapies, drawing on the latest medical research, presented in an easy reference format. £2.99.

Herbal First Aid by Andrew Chevallier BA, MNIMH. A beautifully clear reference book of natural remedies and general first aid in the home. £2.99.

Natural Taste – Herbal Teas, A Guide for Home Use by Andrew Chevallier BA, MNIMH. This charmingly illustrated book contains a comprehensive compendium of Herbal Teas gives information on how to make it, its benefits, history and folklore. £2.99.

Garlic– How Garlic Protects Your Heart by Prof E. Ernst MD, PhD. Used as a medicine for over 4500 years, this book examines the latest scientific evidence supporting Garlic's effect in reducing cardiovascular disease, the Western World's number one killer. £3.99.

Insomnia – Doctor I Can't Sleep by Dr Adrian Williams FRCP. Written by one of the world's leading sleep experts, Dr Williams explains the phenomenon of sleep and sleeping disorders and gives advice on treatment. With 25% of the adult population reporting difficulties sleeping – this book will be essential reading for many. £2.99.

Signs & Symptoms of Vitamin Deficiency by Dr Leonard Mervyn BSc, PhD, C.Chem, FRCS. A home guide for self diagnosis which explains and assesses Vitamin Therapy for the prevention of a wide variety of diseases and illnesses. £2.99.

Causes & Prevention of Vitamin Deficiency by Dr Leonard Mervyn BSc, PhD, C.Chem, FRCS. A home guide to the Vitamin content of foods and the depletion caused by cooking, storage and processing. It includes advice for those whose needs are increased due to lifestyle, illness etc. £2.99.